First published 1983

Macdonald & Co
(Publishers) Ltd
Maxwell House
Worship Street
London EC2A 2EN

© Macdonald & Co
(Publishers) Ltd 1983

ISBN 0 356 07537 0 (cased)
ISBN 0 356 07531 1 (limp)

Made and printed by
Purnell & Sons
(Book Production) Ltd
Paulton, Bristol
Member of BPCC plc

**Editor**
John Morton

**Designer**
John Fitzmaurice

**Production**
Rosemary Bishop

**Picture research**
Peter Harrison

**Consultant**
Dr. Frank Tallett
Lecturer in History
University of Reading

**Illustrators**
Leon Baxter
Dave Eaton
Tony Payne
Richard Hook/Temple Art
(cover)

Aberdeen City Libraries 55C
Antwerp, Musée Royale 26
BPCC/Picturepoint 55B
Bishopsgate Institute 25UC, 25B, 52B
Bridgeman Art Library 9T, 57B
Burnley Public Library 10T
Canterbury Museum, New Zealand 27TL
Jean-Loup Charmet 46T
Chicago Historical Society 31 (both)
Museum of the City of New York 18T, 21B, 33B
Charles Frederic Ulrich: IN THE LAND OF PROMISE—CASTLE GARDEN in the collection of the Corcoran Gallery of Art, Museum Purchase 56B
Arnold H. Crane Collection 36
Deutsches Museum, Munich 13T
Mary Evans Picture Library 14-15T, 23BL, 25T, 25LC, 27B, 32B, 33T, 34T, 34B, 37B, 38CL, 38B, 43C, 46B, 47B, 57C

EdiMedia 35T
E.T. Archive Dunhill Colln. 39T
Fotomas Index 8-9B, 37T
Hirschsprung Colln., Copenhagen 29B
B. Howarth-Loomes 23CR, 42T
BBC Hulton PL 6L 9R, 22-23C, 42B
Illustrated London News Picture Library 15B, 24T, 27C, 56T
Ironbridge Gorge Museum Trust 16T
Konstmuseum, Copenhagen 29T, 35B
Archives, Fried Krupp GmbH 11B
Library of Congress, Washington 16B, 24B, 27TR, 49T
Manchester City Art Gallery 28B
Mansell Collection 13B, 32T, 38CC, 38CR, 43C, 43T, 44T, 48T, 49C, 50T, 51T, 53T
National Maritime Museum 15T
New York, Metropolitan Museum of Art 11T, 18B
Novosti Press Agency 51B
Nürnberg, Stadtgeschichtliche

Museen 16C
Österreichische Galerie, Vienna 17B
People's Palace Museum, Glasgow 23BR
Picturepoint 9C
Ponce, Museo de Arte, 40-41
Popperfoto 14B, 17C, 20B
Preussischer Kulturbesitz 8T, 41B, 53B
Quimper, Musée des Beaux Arts 45T
by gracious permission of Her Majesty the Queen, 5, 44-45B
courtesy, The Salvation Army 19B
Science Museum, London 49B
Sheffield City Museum 30B
Snowdon 21T
Sotheby Parke-Bernet 47T
by perm., Master & Fellows, Trinity College, Cambridge 28T
Roger-Viollet 51C
Walker Art Gallery, Liverpool 10B
Wellcome Institute 37CL, 37CR, 40B
Windsor, Royal Library 50B, 52T

everyday life in the

# Nineteenth Century

E. R. Chamberlin

Macdonald Educational

# The 19th century

The 19th century was like a bridge connecting the past with the present, and the old with the new. At the start of the century, life was not so very different from Roman times–although a Roman would have been rather shocked by the state of the roads and the filthy towns! But by the end of the century, life was not so very different from the world we know today.

In 1800, the only way to travel on land was on your own two legs, or to use an animal. By 1900 steam trains were carrying millions of people at what seemed to be fantastic speeds (express trains went as fast as 150 kph). At sea, in 1800, ships were propelled by wind; if the wind stopped, the ship stopped. Sailors might even die of hunger while they waited for the wind to blow again. By 1900, iron and steel ships steamed the oceans, regardless of whether the wind blew or not.

People's lives changed just as much. In 1800 most people lived in country villages; by 1900 many of them lived and worked in towns. At the start of the century the food they ate came from the garden or a local farm. By the century's end, it might have come from the other side of the world.

Inventors showered the world with new ideas–photography, gas lights, electric motors, gramophones, typewriters, and hundreds more. Today we take these inventions for granted: 19th century people were astonished by these 'marvels of science'.

We are only now, late in the 20th century, learning how to cope with some of the enormous changes of the 19th century. People who lived in the 19th century had to try and adjust to these changes and upheavals as they happened.

# Contents

# The Great Exhibition

In 1851 the world's first international exhibition was held in London. Called *The Great Exhibition of the Works of Industry of All Nations*, it was mainly the idea of Prince Albert, Queen Victoria's husband. He was fascinated by science and industry and was proud of Britain's success. He wanted an international exhibition so that ordinary people could see what other countries had to offer. It was also a chance to prove to others that Britain was the 'workshop of the world'. The exhibition was a 'shop window' to the rest of the world for all the exciting new products streaming from Britain's factories.

The Crystal Palace, the vast building for the exhibition, was itself a wonder. It used brand new building methods: cast iron frames held over 300,000 glass panes. It was so big that 30 metre elm trees grew inside it! Nobody wanted to miss the wonder of the age. In twenty weeks over 6,000,000 people (more than twice London's population) saw the exhibition.

The Great Exhibition was so successful that other countries rushed to hold their own. Between 1851 and 1900 there were forty-one exhibitions in countries such as France, Germany, India, Australia and America. Like the 1851 exhibition, each country hoped its exhibition would be a proud window to the world. If you visited one of these exhibitions, you might see anything from a penknife with eighty blades, to a sewing machine, to a giant steam press, or the latest huge cannon from Germany's Krupp works. But how did all this come about in the first place?

▶ The Medieval Court in the 1851 exhibition. This style of Gothic building and furniture was very popular in the century, especially for churches. Exhibitions concentrated on mechanical and scientific wonders, but gradually more artistic exhibits, national costumes and crafts were shown.

▼ A wonder of science! Visitors marvelled at technical exhibits like this electric dynamo at the 1891 Frankfurt exhibition. Britain led the industrial world in 1851, but was soon rivalled by Germany and the USA.

▼ Britain's John Bull proudly leads the world to the Crystal Palace (far right). Each person comes from a different country: for example, the man with a tuba is German. America's eagle leads the animals which include Britain's lion (arm-in-arm with the Prussian eagle and French cock) and the Russian bear.

12 February 1889

10 May 1888

9 September 1887

▲ New York's 1858 exhibition copied the Crystal Palace's design, but not its success. The first Crystal Palace was prefabricated (built from factory-made parts); after the exhibition it was taken apart, like a giant kit, and rebuilt 10 km away. In 1936 it too burnt down.

▲ Each international exhibition tried to be bigger and better than the ones before. For the 1889 Paris exhibition, Gustave Eiffel built his famous tower to attract the crowds.

# The Industrial Revolution

In the early 1800s England was changing in a new way. Hungry steam engines (fed from huge coal deposits) drove clattering new labour-saving machines. Businessmen's profits bought more machines to make even more profits. We call this process, which began in England, the Industrial Revolution. Life would never be the same again.

It began with cloth. Cloth was made in different stages: wool or cotton was prepared, spun, dyed and, finally, woven. Workers specialized in just one of these jobs and did it at home. This way, they made more than if each worker did all the different jobs. But bosses could not control the quality or quantity of homemade cloth, so they wanted to oversee the work under one roof (a factory). There, workers minding expensive machines produced hundreds of times as much cloth as home-workers using just their muscles and simple tools.

Unlike many Europeans, few English poor had land on which to grow food to eat or exchange for other things. So, millions of these people had to work for others, for *money*. Their wages bought factory goods – without them, the factories would have been pointless. It was these same people who were able to leave the country to live and work in the towns and factories.

New machines and factories led to more inventions and factories. Businessmen made huge profits. Their success

▲ This little girl worked in a cotton mill. Most workers in these sorts of factories were children or women. They had nimbler hands than men and could reach into the machines to clean them. Working conditions were terrible, and children often worked twelve or more hours a day.

▼ An English coal pit-head in about 1820 with a steam winding engine. Without steam power, the Industrial Revolution could not have happened. By the 1780s James Watt found a way to make the up-and-down motion of a steam piston drive a wheel. Using connecting belts, steam engines drove the new factory machines.

encouraged more people to start businesses. Their growing number swelled the size of the middle-class, the people who were between the very rich (the upper-class) and the poor (the working-class).

Eventually, industrialization spread to Europe. Belgium led, but France and Germany followed closely. By 1870 Germany rivalled Britain and the USA produced more than all of Europe together. But the spread was patchy. Spain hardly changed at all while Italy's north became industrialized, but its south stayed peaceful, rural and poor.

▼ *Forging the Shaft,* 1877. This painting shows an American steel works, 75 km north of New York. Despite new machinery and giant steam presses, heavy industry needed heavy work. In the Krupp's factories below, the men would have done similar work.

► The Krupp's armaments and steel works in Germany's Ruhr valley, 1870. By now regions like the Ruhr, northern France, Belgium, and northern England were dominated by factories and mills belching out filthy smoke from their chimneys. Compare how rapidly things had changed since the almost peaceful painting on the left, only fifty years earlier.

# Roads and canals

Early 19th century road travel was painfully slow and unreliable. Most roads were dusty, stony tracks that became impassable bogs in winter. Engineers like Thomas Telford and John Macadam tackled this problem by building roads with firm foundations, good drainage, and hard-wearing surfaces. Later, roads were further improved with asphalt surfaces; by 1858 these were a common sight in Paris. Inns (called stages) along the new roads supplied fresh horses so people could travel rapidly on regular coaches at average speeds of 16 kph.

Who paid for the building and repairing of these roads? A common solution was to divide roads into sections run by companies which charged tolls when travellers entered a section. But that was inefficient and by the middle of the century most European countries had abandoned it. Gradually, governments began to realize that roads should be built, run, and paid for with public money and taxes.

Before the railways came, water transport was the only way early factories could move bulky goods cheaply and quickly. By the 1830s most European countries had canal networks; the Scheldt canal linked eastern Belgium with the North Sea and in 1840 a German-built canal along the river Rhine joined Switzerland and Belgium.

Roads and canals gave Europe its first efficient transport system since Roman times. But their reign was brief – soon they were threatened by railways. British roads and canals, which were privately run, suffered badly. In the rest of Europe canals fared better; many of them were partly paid for by governments which helped prevent them from falling into disuse.

▲ **English locks. Barges going up hill entered the lowest lock. Water from the next lock was let into it until the barge floated up to the level of the next lock. By repeating this, the barge got to the top of the hill–in this case 18 m above the lowest lock. It was a very slow system which took only one barge at a time. In the rest of Europe, new machinery, like the lift below, did the same job, but much more quickly.**

**British canals could hardly compete with the railways and little was spent improving them. Today most are tourist attractions or in ruins.**

▼ **An 1890 Belgian barge lift. European canals could carry much larger barges than British ones could. By 1874, French barges had to be a minimum weight of 350 tonnes; British barges were averaging only 25 tonnes. Wide rivers, like the Rhine, helped European canals to remain vital routes.**

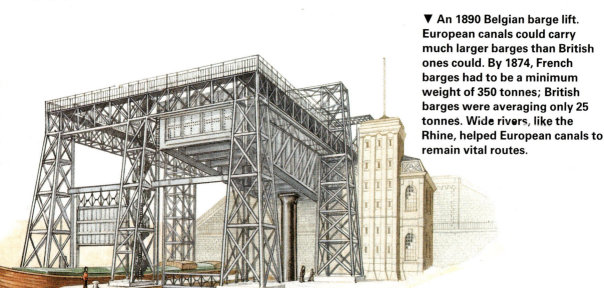

gravel

60 mm stones

65 mm stones

175-225 mm of
large
foundation
stones

subsoil

▲ Karl Benz, a German inventor, with one of the first spluttering motor cars. For many years a car was just a rich person's toy. In the 20th century cars eventually caused the decline of railways.

◄ A stage coach pays at a toll gate. Though stage coaches had a short life before the railways came, the British system was envied by Europeans for its speed. Young men often paid extra for the thrill of riding beside the driver. Beneath the road is a cross-section showing how Thomas Telford built his roads.

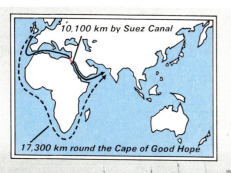

10,100 km by Suez Canal

17,300 km round the Cape of Good Hope

The Suez Canal was built between 1859 and 1869. Sailing ships could not use it—the wind did not always blow in the right direction. Trade between Europe and the eastern colonies was expanding; the map shows how the canal shortened the routes. One result of the canal was to make Indian cotton cheaper to ship and it could now compete with American cotton as raw material for Britain's thriving cloth industry.

# Ships and shipping

In 1800 it took up to eight weeks to cross the Atlantic; by 1900 it took about a week. Emigrants seeking new lives abroad; officials off to run the colonies; food to feed Europe's and America's growing population; exports from Europe's booming factories: all these created a huge growth in shipping.

Sailing ships were very efficient, so it was a long time before they were challenged by the unreliable new steam ships. The clipper *Cutty Sark*, for example, built in 1869, worked until the 1930s. Clippers (they 'clipped' time off voyages) raced valuable cargoes like Chinese tea and Australian wool to Europe and America.

In 1838 a race for the first steam ship to cross the Atlantic was won by the *Sirius*. But she had a four day start. Her rival, Brunel's *Great Western* paddle steamer, lost by only three and a half hours, at an average speed of 16.3 kph. Early steam ships needed valuable cargo space to store coal and fresh water for the boilers. Engines were unreliable and often blew up. But, slowly, steam replaced sail and by 1874 over 75% of ships were steam-driven. Made of iron, and later of steel, steamships were not only stronger and faster, but could be built much larger than sailing ships. As a result, shipping costs tumbled. In 1874 it cost twenty cents to ship a bushel of grain across the Atlantic; by 1904 it cost two cents.

Ships could not carry enough coal for long trips. Coaling stations, like Montevideo in South America and Durban in South Africa, grew up to refuel ships' bunkers.

▲ Britain had the world's largest merchant fleet; much of it was built in these Clyde shipyards. To protect her ships and keep shipping routes open, Britain ruled the waves with the world's largest navy.

◄ Marseilles, France, about 1860. Increased international trade caused ports like Marseilles, New York, Hamburg, Rotterdam, Liverpool and Genoa to expand rapidly.

Wooden ships had a maximum size, beyond which they sagged in the middle. So, many more wooden ships than iron ships were needed to carry the same amount of cargo. Busy ports were a forest of sailing ship masts.

▲ Brunel's *Great Eastern* being built in 1857, in London. At 17,160 tonnes, no bigger ship was built until 1901. She could carry 10,900 tonnes of coal and 4,000 passengers. Technically too far ahead of her time, she was a commercial failure.

▼ The *Great Eastern*'s first-class saloon. Whether you went first-class or steerage (deep inside the ship, the worst and cheapest place to be), you could not escape storms.

# Railways

▼ Navvies (short for navigators) building a railway cutting in 1847. These skilled, hardworking men had only gunpowder and their own muscles to build the railways (years later, steam shovels would ease their work). These men travelled abroad from Britain to help build some of the rest of Europe's first railways.

An English writer once said that people who lived before the railways were 'like Father Noah and his family out of the Ark'. Certainly, railways changed everything. They moved goods cheaply from factory to shop. They opened up isolated areas of Europe that could now specialize in what they farmed best and sell it cheaply to the rest of Europe. Without railways, an Industrial Revolution would have been impossible.

No one person invented the railway. Instead, over many years, different ideas were combined until the railway emerged. The first *wooden* railways ran in mines so that horses could drag heavier wagons than on rough ground. In the 1800s France and England experimented with steampowered road machines. But it was not until 1813 that George

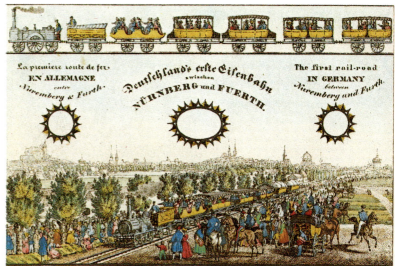

La premiere route de fer EN ALLEMAGNE entre Nuremberg & Furth

Deutschland's erste Eisenbahn zwischen NÜRNBERG und FUERTH.

The first rail-road IN GERMANY between Nuremberg and Furth.

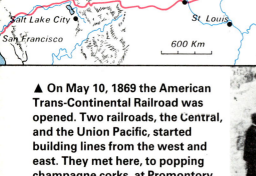

▲ On May 10, 1869 the American Trans-Continental Railroad was opened. Two railroads, the Central, and the Union Pacific, started building lines from the west and east. They met here, to popping champagne corks, at Promontory Point. The line opened up the vast American continent to thousands of settlers and farmers who could now send millions of cattle to the big cities and Europe.

Stephenson's 'locomotive' reliably pulled heavy, 30 tonne, loads along iron rails.

The world's first public train steamed out of Darlington on September 27, 1825. From then, Britain's railways mushroomed: in 1843 there were 3,200 kilometres of tracks, by 1870 there were 22,000 kilometres. At first rich landowners feared the snorting iron dragons would terrify their cows and stop them milking. But when they saw the money to be made, they joined in the 'railway mania', scrambling to buy railway company shares or sell land for huge profits. Fortunes were made; many were lost.

Continental railways developed more sensibly, mainly because they were longer and more expensive to build. In France and Italy lines were owned by the state and rented to private companies. German railways, too, got state aid. By the 1900s most European railways were state run: this did not happen in Britain until 1948.

◄ The first German railway was opened in 1835 from Nuremburg to Fürth. Europe was not slow to follow Britain's example; by 1850 the rest of Europe had 24,000 km of railway tracks and by 1870, 104,000 km of tracks.

▼ The painting shows the inside of a railway terminus in Austria's capital, Vienna. The photograph shows its outside. Railways often made more money than other 19th century companies. They wanted to show off their success and they often did this by building huge, extravagantly decorated stations in the big cities. Many, like this one, or London's St Pancras station, looked more like Gothic cathedrals than railway stations.

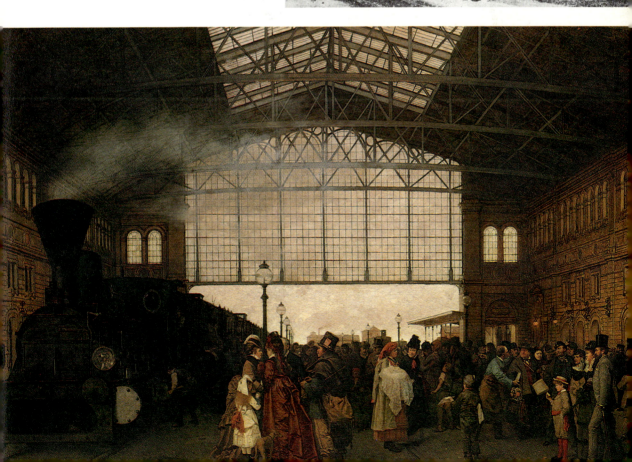

# Families

People thought families were vitally important. They loved their children, but demanded respect and obedience in return. They hoped that family loyalties and a 'proper upbringing' would make their children grow up into responsible and successful adults. Books like Mrs Isabella Beeton's *Book of Household Management* and an American book, *Fifteen Cent Dinners for Workingmen's Families*, were written to help people run their homes and families well.

Rich parents' young children were looked after by a nurse. They spent much of their time in a nursery where they could read colour picture books or the first pop-up books; *The Speaking Picturebook* even made the sound of an animal on a page as you pulled a tab. If books bored children, German clockwork trains, French china dolls, or educational jigsaws might amuse them. Governesses often gave children their first lessons at home. When he was old enough, a boy might join his father's business. His sisters helped at home, learning to become 'ladies' by practising the piano, embroidery, or dancing, while waiting for 'suitable' husbands.

▼ A very rich American family relaxes at home. Houses were large enough for grandparents to live in the same building. The children on the right are doing a jigsaw.

◀ 'Street arabs' (poor children with no home). Hot air from a baker's oven came up through the railings that they are sleeping on. This picture was taken in New York in the 1890s, but all cities had homeless children who had run away from cruel masters or whose parents had died.

Rich wives did not go out to work in case others thought their husbands could not afford to keep them. Instead, they ran the household. It was a major task organizing the servants, but it was one of the few responsible jobs women were given. Most women visited friends in their spare time. Others did 'charitable work' (helping the poor). This might lead to other work in local affairs. Slowly, women were becoming independent of men.

Poor people loved their children too, but it was much harder to look after a poor family. Many families who had worked together at home now worked in factories. Children might work in a different factory from their parents. Those who were too young to work (they often began at five years old) might be left with a minder who gave them bits of bread soaked in milk and water tied up in a dirty rag. Worse still, minders used 'infant preservatives' which contained drugs to make a child sleepy. But slowly, wages rose and many parents no longer had to force their children out to work. When working hours got shorter, people had more time to take children on outings or even holidays.

▼ A poor family at work in the 1890s. Goods like brushes, cigars or matchboxes, could not be made by machines. Instead, they were made by people working long hours at home for little pay.

# The home

If you could afford it, your house had servants. Even a small house had a 'maid-of-all-work', who slept in the attic. A rich family might be outnumbered by its servants, each with a special job. A humble servant's life was hard. She rose at 4.30 am and worked until 10.00 pm when she fell exhausted into bed. She probably sat down only to eat lunch or clean the silver. Coal was cheap, each room had a fire, so she spent much of her time heaving coal upstairs and ashes downstairs. Sunday was a rest day when she got up half an hour later and went to bed half an hour earlier. Sometimes she had an afternoon off. For this, in 1860, she might earn £10 a year.

Despite her harsh life, it was better than she could expect in the country, where most servants came from. She 'saw the world' and could hope to rise to a better job. She would hope to find a husband from a slightly better class than her own.

The factories produced so many cheap goods that people could afford things that used to be luxuries. Carpets and curtains, for example, were now found in quite ordinary homes. Gas lighting was used early in the 1800s and eventually working people could afford it. But bathrooms were still thought a luxury for the poor; most people bathed in zinc tubs in front of the fire. Lavatories in poor areas were outside and often shared by a hundred or more people.

Few people owned their houses; most rented them instead. Richer people paid every three months or once a year. Poorer people paid weekly; if they fell behind with the rent, they were thrown out onto the street.

▲ A servant struggles with the latest home labour-saving device–an 1880 mangle. Only the rich could afford washing machines and similar appliances.

► This London house is kept just as it was over eighty years ago. This is the drawing room. Linley Sambourne, the rich artist who lived here, drew the original black and white cartoons on pages 53 and 54.

► Many poor families, like this New York one in the 1880s, lived in just one room. As well as the four people here, a baby slept on a pile of old rags. Father heaved coal on the docks; 'when work was fairly brisk', he said, he earned about $5 a week.

► The cook (centre) with her 'slaveys' (maid servants) from a large house. With so many women as this, this 1886 house probably had as many male staff again, including a butler, gardeners and a coach driver. Even by Victorian standards this was a rich household. Servants got free board and lodging and some wages as well. A 14 year old under-housemaid in 1884 earned about 20p a week–which would have bought a dozen eggs, a kilo of sausages and a kilo of cheese.

# Fashion and clothes

Fashion changed beyond recognition during the century. Early in the 1800s men wore bright and fancy clothes. By the 1840s a well-dressed man was beginning to wear darker clothes. He had clothes for every occasion; a fashion book insisted that he have four top-coats (a morning coat, a frock coat, a dress coat and an overcoat) as well as seven pairs of trousers and five waistcoats!

Clothes showed how successful (or unsuccessful!) a person was. Hats were a sure way to tell which class a man belonged to: upper- and middle-class men wore top hats; a working man might wear a bowler (known as 'billy-cocks'). Poor men

*A French postman*

*A British railway worker*

▲ **A new sight was civilian uniforms (military uniforms had been common for a long time). Thousands of people worked on the railways (900,000 in 1881 in Britain), in the police force or for the post office. Smart uniforms let everyone recognize who these important people were.**

▼ **These pictures show some of the changes in fashion between the beginning and the end of the century by which time clothes were not so very different from those of today.**

*1800: A husband and wife off to the theatre. Men wore shoes instead of boots and put macassar oil in their hair. Armchairs had antimacassars to keep hair oil off them. The wife wears a crinoline.*

*1895: Women's suits had tight waists, often with a bustle (all that was left of the crinoline, from which it developed) behind. Sailor suits were popular for children, as were bloomers for sporty young women.*

*1800: Men still wore boots, but not fancy wigs. Women wore loose, flimsy 'empire' dresses that would have been suitable for a much hotter climate. At no other time in the century did women wear so little. Later, they tortured themselves in tight corsets.*

made hats from old clothes or even folded them from paper. Very poor heads went bare.

New factory-made dyes, mauvine and alazarine, made women's clothes much brighter. Mauve was so popular that the 1890s were called the Mauve Decade. In 1862, an American, Amelia Bloomer, designed a sensible trouser-like costume called 'bloomers'. It was angrily ridiculed. Few women wore her invention until the bicycling craze.

Working people wore much the same as their grandparents did, especially in the country where farm workers could be recognized by their traditional smocks. But cheap imported clothes from Germany did allow working people to be a lot smarter—even if only on Sundays. Boots were always an expensive item and underclothing remained a luxury for the very poor.

▼ Putting on a crinoline in five easy stages. Business boomed in the 50s and it was mirrored in bigger and bigger skirts needing more and more petticoats to hold them up. By the mid-50s, skirts were too heavy to wear, so crinolines were invented. Made of whalebone or springy steel, they stayed in fashion until the mid-60s.

No respectable woman showed even her ankles; to avoid doing so, women often wore pantaloons under crinolines. These pictures were used in stereoscopes (page 42).

◀ A cotton mill. Wool was very expensive; cheap factory-made cotton allowed working people to dress much better than ever before. Women's clothes often had bright, printed patterns.

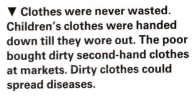

▼ Clothes were never wasted. Children's clothes were handed down till they wore out. The poor bought dirty second-hand clothes at markets. Dirty clothes could spread diseases.

# Food and drink

Improved European farming and cheap food imports from countries like the USA gave people better and more varied food. From the 1870s onwards, refrigerated ships carried meat from the vast Australian and American plains to Europe's cities. In America, by about 1850, H.J. Heinz was bottling his garden horseradish. Soon he used a French idea to can his '57 Varieties' for the American Civil War armies. Canning allowed food produced in one part of the world to be eaten much later elsewhere. Tea, coffee and cocoa fell in price and helped reduce the amount of alcohol people drank. Sugar, once a luxury, sweetened these drinks.

Food was not always pure. People were poisoned by things added to food to improve its looks or make it stretch further. Red lead was added to cheese to colour it, acid to wine, chalk to flour, and water to milk.

People still preferred meat and puddings to fresh vegetables and fruit. But they had more money to spend on food and were slowly becoming healthier. American tailors, for example, found that young men were a centimetre or so taller than their fathers.

Even the lavish habits of the rich changed. Chefs, unemployed after the French Revolution, opened restaurants or went abroad. Dining-out and French food became the fashion and even simple foods had French names—fried chicken became *les filets de volaille à la maréchal*.

THE "ALBIONETTE"

▲ Part of an advertisement for an 1897 oil stove. It cost £4.50, about twice as much as a labourer earned a week. The advertisement boasted that it could be run 'at one-third the cost of coal or gas', but it would have been expensive for poor people.

▶ Many poor people could not afford a stove or coal to burn on it—they probably did not even have room for one. Often, there was no clean water for cooking. Instead, people often took food to bakers who cooked it in their ovens.

PORK CUTTING
FIRST OPERATION
REMOVING
HAMS and SHOULDERS
SPLITTING RIBS
SWIFT & COMPANY

◀ A Chicago meat factory. Like many other industries, much food production was done in factories. Not only could butchery be speeded up in a factory, but waste from carcasses – bones, skin, fat, and so on – could be used to make extra profits. This factory made 4,000 kg of sausage a day and had 160,000 kg vats for turning fat into soap. Most of the pigs and cattle farmed in their millions on the great American plains went to Chicago for slaughter and packing.

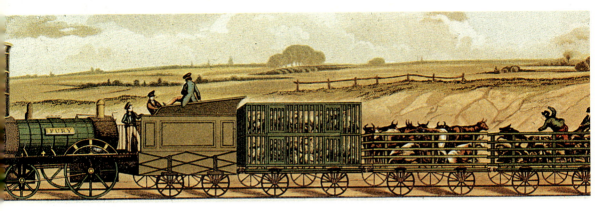

▲ Without railways, it would have been impossible to transport enough food to feed the people in the growing cities. So, without railways, cities could never have grown as big as they did.

▲ A hot potato seller. People worked long hours and might walk ten km, or more, to work each day. Small wonder that they had no time or energy to cook meals. In busy streets you would hear people offering all sorts of things to eat; pies, lemonade, coffee, soup and many more.

▶ 'Buy my fresh milk, fresh, warm milk from the cow!' Milk goes bad so quickly that until there were fast refrigerated trains, dairy cows were kept in or very near the cities where milk was sold.

# Farming

Europe's population more than doubled to 400,000,000 between 1800 and 1900. Only a revolution in farming methods could begin to feed the extra mouths. Changes in farming began in England around 1700 and slowly spread to Europe and other parts of the world by the 19th century.

Farms produced *more*, with *less* human work, in many different ways. Many poor farmers had split their farms between their sons so farms became smaller and produced less. In the 19th century many of these tiny farms were merged into bigger and more efficient farms. Farmers bred fatter, meatier animals, sheep with more wool, and cows which gave more milk. Many of these animals were the parents of 'superherds' abroad. Tools improved, ranging from the humble, but vital, scythe to machines like seed drills which meant less seeds were needed to grow crops.

By the 1870s cheap food from abroad began to flood into Europe. European farms had to change to compete. Before this, most farms grew a bit of everything. By specializing in one sort of farming, farms produced much more, more cheaply. But it meant more cheese, for example, was made than could be sold locally. Only the railways could get the cheese to far off, hungry cities. Denmark and Holland changed from grain to dairy farming. Pigs and chickens are easy to keep on a dairy farm and by 1900 Denmark was selling eggs and bacon to Britain. Other areas specialized in fruit or vegetables.

The farming revolution made many workers redundant. Food prices fell, so farmworkers were paid less. Rather than starve, millions left for town jobs or emigrated.

▲ *The Flax Field* (Flax was used to make an expensive hard-wearing cloth called linen). This Dutch painting of 1887 shows that, despite new machines, life for most farm workers was hard, back-breaking labour. Women and children often did lighter tasks such as planting seedlings or picking crops.

▶ An Irish potato riot. In 1845 and 1846 potato blight caused widespread crop failures in parts of Europe. Irish peasants ate almost nothing but potatoes and could not afford any other food. Many died of starvation, while others emigrated to America. By the end of the century about 10,500,000 Irish had left their homeland.

▲ At the top is a New Zealand steam thresher. Steam ploughing was done with a stationary engine which dragged a plough on chains across a field. Most machinery, though, was still horse-drawn, like the 1887 American combine harvester below drawn by 33 horses. Machines cut down the work in farming and, so, the cost of food.

▶ A cartoon of rich Russian landowners gambling with bundles of their serfs. Serfs worked on their owner's land and earned no wages. They could be sold with the owner's land – it was almost slavery. Russia finally abolished it in 1861, though earlier in the century much of Europe, including Poland and Prussia, had serfs. Countries that kept serfdom the longest were often slow to industrialize.

# Earning a living

The new industries and factories needed new skills. There were many new ways to earn a living. For example, skilled men worked as engine-drivers, mechanics, or electricians. But the Industrial Revolution condemned millions more people to a harsh new way of life.

In the past people worked at their own pace (depending on the weather and time of the year) in or near their homes. Now factory workers were forced to start work and finish at regular times, day in, day out, year in, year out. Machines stopped only for maintenance. A factory owner had to make the most of his expensive machines, so he made his workers work appallingly long hours. Twelve, fourteen and more hours a day was normal. If you did not like it, plenty of jobless people were willing to take your job beside the machine.

Women and children were worst off. Children as young as five years minded machines, snatching only a few minutes for lunch. Children in mines were less lucky. Deep mines needed ventilation. Children sat in damp, lonely darkness opening and closing shutters to keep the air moving.

In England publicity about child sweeps caused an outrage. Before the sweeps climbed the filthy, narrow chimneys, they were 'prepared' for work. A master rubbed salt water into a child's knees and elbows by a hot fire until the limbs bled. Repeating this eventually hardened the skin. Reluctantly, governments in many countries abolished the worst abuses of workers like this.

▲ An English coal pit-brow girl in 1867. Women usually did lighter work, but some did work as hard as the men's, shifting coal in, or above, the mines. Women did similar work in French and Belgian mines.

▶ Part of a painting called *Work*. Most middle- and upper-class Victorians believed that work improved you and was 'good for the soul'. Perhaps this helped them excuse some of the horrors of the factories. The workers in this painting reflect this attitude with their handsome, noble and healthy faces. The reality was rather different as the Italian painting (far right) of a hatter shows. (There was an outrage when this painting was shown. People complained that it was too 'realistic'; they were especially angered by the dripping nose.)

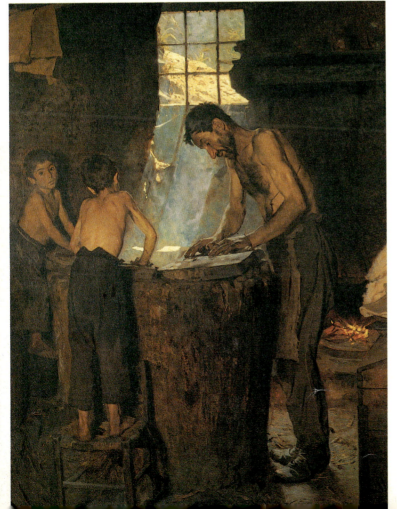

▲ *The Wounded Workman* (a Swedish miner). Industrial accidents, diseases and deaths were horrifyingly common: for example, between 1856 and 1866, one thousand British miners died *each* year from accidents. For each recorded death by accident, there would have been even more unrecorded deaths from 'miners' lung' (caused by inhaling coal dust): long before he died from it, a miner would have been sacked because he could not breathe well enough to do his job.

Until governments made laws against it, machines had no guards on them to stop hands getting caught in the whirring machinery.

Few employers realized, or cared, that some of the materials their workers used were dangerous, such as phosphrous, which was used to make matches. The Mad Hatter in *Alice in Wonderland* is based on hatters who used mercury to make hat felt. Mercury fumes damaged their brains.

# The growth of cities

Many towns and cities grew explosively as people came to live and work in them. In 1800 only 22 European towns had more than 100,000 people; America had nothing this big. By 1900 Europe had 84 towns this size or bigger and America had 53. For the first time ever, there were cities of a million people or more. London was the largest (6,500,000), followed by Paris and Berlin.

Some ancient cities, like Lyons in France, grew with trade and industry. Many new cities developed through industry, but there were other causes. Chicago grew so big because it was a centre for the farm produce—meat, wheat and timber—from the western USA. Rotterdam, Europe's busiest seaport, expanded to 400,000 by 1900.

Many cities, like Chicago, did not exist at all before 1800. In one case, a town grew overnight. Oklahoma, in the USA, was founded on April 22, 1889; by the next day 100,000 settlers had rushed in to stake a land claim.

Land in city centres was expensive. Many office buildings had to grow upwards; by 1891 New York had a steel-framed 21 storey skyscraper with an electric lift.

England led in the spread of cities; by 1851 more people lived in towns than the country. In Germany this happened by 1890 and in America not until 1920. Elsewhere, cities spread more slowly. In 1900 most Europeans were still country people, and only 40% of France's and 25% of Scandinavia's population lived in towns

▶ By 1870 Chicago was a huge, busy city. But in 1820, it was just a few huts by a river (small picture below); it is the same river in both pictures. Chicago's growth was mainly due to the meat factories. Like many American cities, Chicago was neatly planned on a grid with streets running at right angles to each other.

▼ Sheffield in 1854 was Britain's major steel-producing city. Its population in 1801 was 46,000; by 1901 it was over eight times bigger. Like many other industrial cities, Sheffield grew rapidly with no attempts to plan its growth.

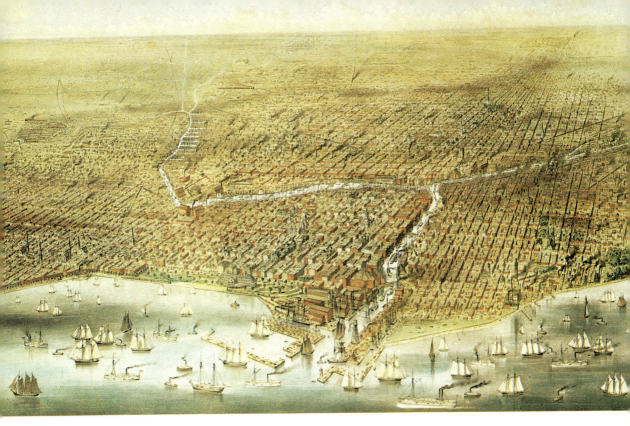

▼ Any city could have had a map like this. As cities grew, more of their poor squeezed into old houses, causing more of them to die. By the 1870s, much of old Paris was rebuilt. Grand houses for the rich on wide streets *(boulevards)* replaced rotten slums. But nobody built new homes for the slum-dwellers who had been forced to move out to make way for the new buildings.

## Overcrowding in Paris, 1886-1891

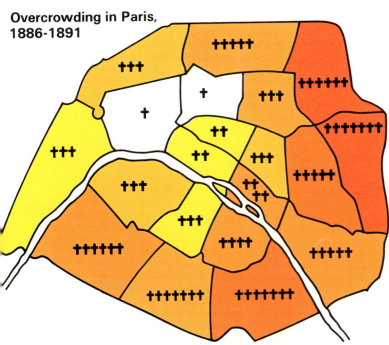

| Numbers of deaths per 1,000 people each year. | |
|---|---|
| † | 14 |
| †† | 17 |
| ††† | 20 |
| †††† | 22 |
| ††††† | 25 |
| †††††† | 28 |
| ††††††† | 31 |
| Amount of people living more than two to a room. | |
| | 5.5% |
| | 8.0% |
| | 10.7% |
| | 13.4% |
| | 16.1% |
| | 18.7% |
| | 21.4% |

# Life in the cities

Cities grew so big, so quickly, that it was almost impossible to provide essential things like clean water and sewers. London enlarged its sewers in the 1840s but still pumped waste into the river Thames. Parliament had to close down once because the stench of the river made members ill. Filthy streets caused many outbreaks of disease–cholera in particular.

Mean little houses were hurriedly, shoddily built for city workers. There were few building regulations and houses were often built back-to-back in narrow alleys with little sunlight or fresh air. Some rooms had no windows.

Burning coal powered steam trains and factory engines and heated houses; cities were often under a permanent smoke cloud. In the past, rich and poor lived in the same areas, but late in the century many rich people moved to leafy garden suburbs, safe from the filthy squalor of poor areas.

But all was not gloom. Many cities had parks or zoos, like London's Green Park or Berlin's *Tiergarten*, to relieve the filthy grime. Other cities, like Paris, Vienna and Brussels were less industrial and escaped the pea-soup fogs that choked cities like London. Parisians delighted to relax outside cafés sipping a drink; few Londoners would have risked it.

The invention of coal gas lights in about 1800 and electric lights in the 1880s meants that, for the first time, streets were lit at night. So were the large department stores which were built from the 1840s onwards. Shopping arcades for the rich were built in every city. These were streets covered with glass on iron frames. Inside you could window shop for rich silks or delicate German china, safe and dry and away from the street noise and smell.

▲ This photograph was taken in Glasgow in 1868, but many of Europe's poor lived in similar overcrowded and unhealthy slums.

◄ Many parts of cities were badly lit and dangerous to walk in. Crime was common. This 1856 cartoon makes fun of this (and the crinoline fashion!) by suggesting 'antigarrotting' (anti-strangling) clothing for men.

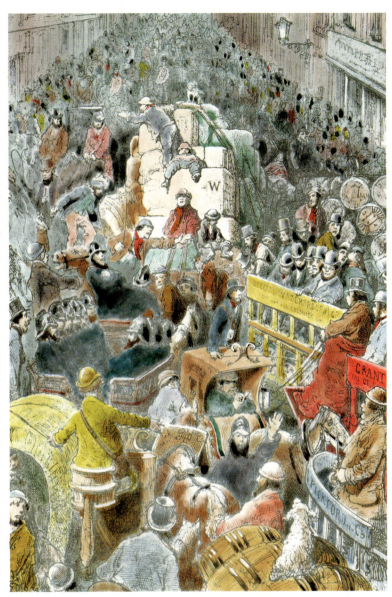

◄ A London traffic jam in 1872. Charles Dickens described a jam like this in *Nicholas Nickleby* as 'vehicles of all shapes and sizes . . . in one moving mass like running water'. Cities needed more and more horses to carry the people and goods that daily came in by railway. People walked or took horse-drawn cabs, buses or trams. The rich had private carriages. Freight went on horse-drawn waggons. London in the 1890s had 116,600 horses, which produced 400,000 tonnes of manure a year.

Towards the end of the century, city roads could no longer cope. The solution to the problem was to build railways *inside* cities. But there was no land left for new tracks, so in 1863 London built an underground steam railway. New York (below), Berlin and Düsseldorf built railways above the streets, By 1900, Paris, Vienna and other cities began building electric underground railways.

# Crime and the misfits

◀ A 'rough'; many people thought that criminals were born as criminals. Some 'scientists' even believed they could recognize criminals by the shapes of their skulls!

▼ Not only was it harder to control city crime than country crime, but there was more of it. British crime went up by eight times from 1805 to 1848. Crime rose when business slumped and jobs were scarce.

Factories made a few people wealthy, but impoverished millions of others. Poverty hit the city poor hardest. Country people suffered harsh masters and famines–in an Italian famine peasants ate hay. But peasants could poach, gather firewood, or eat wild fruit; city poor could not. If your work was not needed, you were instantly sacked. No social security helped the jobless, homeless, or sick. Many people thought that the poor were poor through laziness–anyway, the working-classes had to be 'kept in their place' to stop them 'getting above themselves' and stopping the disciplined, smooth-running factories.

Governments helped little, but punished a lot. For example, British workhouses sheltered the destitute. But governments, terrified of encouraging 'idlers', made sure that people feared the workhouse and would do anything to keep out.

Most people lived honest lives, though some sank to amazing depths to get money–people even collected dogs' dung to sell to leather tanners. But some finally turned to crime. To replace the army and night watchmen, Britain set up the world's first police force in 1829 and Europe soon followed. Punishments were harsh. In 1800 Britain had over 200 hanging offences including shoplifting, stealing bread, burning corn ricks, or wrecking one of the new factory machines–governments were worried that workers would revolt against the new factories.

◄ A Paris soup kitchen. Many poor and homeless starved or froze to death. Religious groups, like the French Sisters of Charity and the British Salvation Army, saw that this was not the fault of the poor and set up soup kitchens and cheap hostels. By the end of the century, such efforts made governments begin to take over the duty of helping the poor.

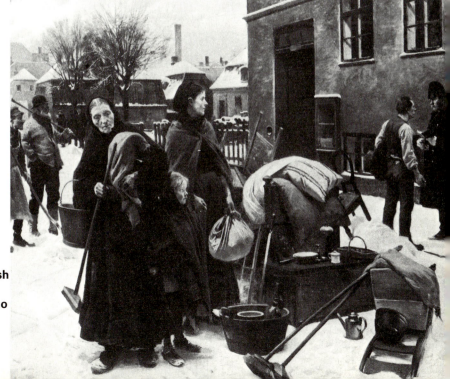

► *Evicted Tenants.* This Swedish painting of 1892 shows the painful fate awaiting people who fell behind with their rent.

# Health and medicine

In the 1830s cholera killed 100,000 French people; in 1849 it killed 16,000 Londoners. Cholera ravaged Europe. A London doctor realised that dirty water carried cholera, but most people ignored him until 1891, when the disease hit Hamburg. Hamburg had dirty water, but nearby Altona had works to clean its water; it was untouched. The solution was clear: clean water supplies defeated cholera.

Cramped, dirty cities bred killer diseases like smallpox, scarlet fever and typhus. Germ-laden water and festering rubbish attracted flies, whose next stop for food might be a baby's plate. Some people had to take turns to use a bed, and so they passed on their typhus-carrying fleas.

Few town people ate enough fruit or vegetables (for

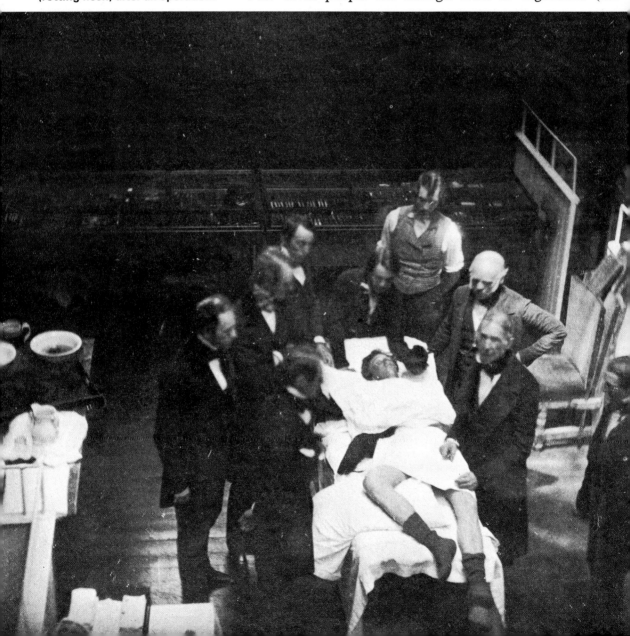

▼ An operation in America using anaesthetics (pain-killing drugs) in 1846. Before anaesthetics, patients were often made drunk so they might not notice the pain of an operation. Usually, if you had a leg sawn off, you died from shock and loss of blood rather than from what was wrong with your leg. Later, doctors like Lister in Scotland used antiseptics to stop people dying from gangrene (rotting flesh) after an operation.

vitamin C). Some got scurvey; country people ate enough greenery (they could afford little else) to avoid it. Many children had bow legs from ricketts, which softens the bones and is caused by too little sunshine and a poor diet.

In most families, at least one child died before its fifth birthday. But, slowly, life improved. Cheap soap and washable cotton clothes kept people cleaner. Water and sewage systems and housing improved gradually. Discoveries, like Pasteur's of how diseases spread, made medicine more effective. As the century wore on, death rates began to fall.

Women had babies at home. For most women, especially poor women, it was an agony; one woman in four died giving birth. Families were large; the idea of contraception was a scandal and abortions were illegal. A woman exhausted by too many babies could visit a back street 'doctor' who, for a fee, got rid of an unwanted baby. These illegal quacks killed thousands of mothers as well as babies.

▼ Improved hygiene and better living conditions probably saved more lives than any medical advances. Efficient sewers were the most important improvements. These are London sewers being laid in 1845. Paris got its first proper sewers when Haussman rebuilt the city with 500 km of sewers. Below the sewer picture is an angry 1828 cartoon showing 'monster soup' (London's filthy water) through a microscope.

▼ For hundreds of years doctors offered little useful or cheap medicine. In desperation, people turned to quack doctors, like this Italian, who sold useless and often dangerous 'cures'.

◀ Florence Nightingale was shocked at the state of the hospitals when she arrived in Turkey to look after injured British soldiers in the Crimean War. She cleaned up the rat-infested wards and made sure her patients were properly fed and looked after. She helped turn hospitals into places people could enter and expect to leave again, alive. She also made nursing one of the few respectable careers for educated women.

In 1872 Eadweard Muybridge used 12 cameras to photograph this horse. Until then, galloping horses had been painted with their legs in impossible positions (like the horses on page 55). These photographs and other inventions led to the first public movie show in 1895, 59 years after a Frenchman took the first still photograph.

# Communications

Five minutes after the 1871 Derby horserace in England, the winner's name was received 8,000 kilometres away in Calcutta, India. The electric telegraph (first used to control railways) sent news instantaneously. The *Great Eastern* laid the first trans-Atlantic cable in 1865 and by 1900 most of the world was cable-linked. Businessmen could instantly order new machines and governments could swiftly instruct distant colonies. The world was shrinking.

In the past the only way to send news was to travel in person or send a messenger. In 1840 Britain started the first public postal service–the 'Penny Post'. For one penny a letter could be sent anywhere in the country. In a few years, the number of letters sent doubled to 169,000,000. Other countries soon copied the idea.

'Mr Watson, come here, I want to see you' were the first words ever heard by telephone on March 10 1876 as Alexander Graham Bell talked to his assistant on his new invention. British post office officials thought the idea would not catch on because there were plenty of messenger boys. They were soon proved wrong.

Now news spread a million times faster. Newspapers were eager to print it first and 'scoop' rival papers. London's *Times* was the first steam-printed paper in 1812. The machine was installed secretly to stop printers (who feared for their jobs) wrecking it. Later, automatic machines set type four times faster than hand-setters could. The New York *Daily Graphic* printed the first photograph (of New York slums) in 1880. After the 1830s cheap, popular newspapers challenged the dreary old papers. Books also became cheaper. All of this would have been impossible before mass education. Cheap printing fed a hunger for scandal, news of scientific wonders, or news of distant wars.

▲ Factory mass-production encouraged businessmen to advertise to help sell the goods pouring from their factories. Cheap printing made this possible. By the end of the century, names like *Kodak* (cameras: 'You press the button— we do the rest'), *Nestlés* (chocolate), *Pears* ('Good morning! Have you used Pear's Soap?') and *Heinz's* '57 Varieties' shouted from posters and magazines.

◀ The first successful typewriter was sold in America in 1874. Busy businessmen found that educated women worked better than male clerks and for less money. Along with the telephone, the typewriter gave women another rare career opportunity.

◀ Magazines became so cheap that by the last quarter of the century most people could afford them. The French and Italian papers on the right suggest that tastes then were similar to today's.

# Education

As late as 1887, the Russian Education Minister said 'children of workmen, servants, cooks and washerwomen, small shopkeepers . . . should not be educated above their station'. Most early 19th century ruling classes had similar feelings. They feared that educated workers would revolt against them and the factory owners.

Most poor children went to church schools, if at all. Many parents could not afford to send their children to school–it stopped them earning money. Church schooling was often bad. In 1850, for example, four out of ten young French army recruits could not read.

A few people thought that *all* children should have a good education, not just the rich children. There was also a growing need for educated people to do new, skilled factory jobs. Schools began to teach 'useful' subjects–the '3Rs', *r*eading, *w*riting, *a*rithmetic.

Schooling slowly improved, but it was expensive and un-popular with voting tax-payers. Church leaders, especially in Catholic countries countries like France, Belgium, Italy and Germany, fought bitterly to keep their control of education. But by the 1880s, many European countries had *free, compulsory* education for *all*. Later, new subjects like foreign languages, botany and art were taught. Better education helped fill a growing need for doctors, engineers and civil servants. By 1914, only one in ten young French soldiers could not read.

Girls' schooling was almost ignored until the end of the century when more thought was given to their needs. But even then it was often because governments realized that a man worked harder if his wife fed him well and looked after his home and children. For example, German girls learned the '3Ks' – *Kinder, Küche, Kirche* (children, cooking, church).

▼ A French church school, 1873. Often a poor child's only chance of education was to learn religion, morality and reading in a church or charity school. An English alphabet book began 'A stands for Angel, who praises the Lord; B stands for Bible, that teaches God's word.' Besides reading, these schools taught little of practical use.

▶ Military-style P.E. exercises in 1888. Many pupils, especially city ones, had bad diets and were sickly and weak. Near the end of the century schools, led by Sweden, tried to improve children's health. Rich English schools 'educated boys to be Christians, gentlemen and scholars, in that order'. Rowdy team games were meant to improve 'team spirit'–one Eton game became a riot which the army had to stop. Elsewhere, team games were rare.

► A London museum in 1840. Many people believed in 'self-help', or self-improvement. The growth of museums, public libraries and evening-classes let many working people overcome, in their spare time, bad childhood schooling. It became easier to go to university: new colleges and old universities became more serious.

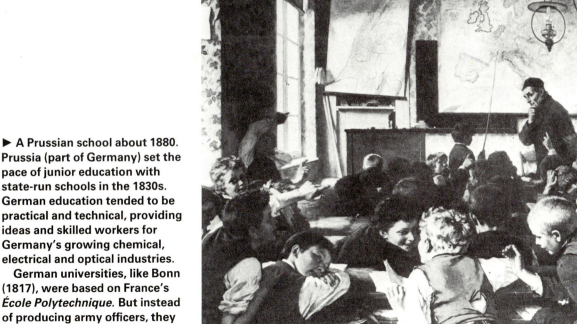

► A Prussian school about 1880. Prussia (part of Germany) set the pace of junior education with state-run schools in the 1830s. German education tended to be practical and technical, providing ideas and skilled workers for Germany's growing chemical, electrical and optical industries.

German universities, like Bonn (1817), were based on France's *École Polytechnique.* But instead of producing army officers, they produced scientists or engineers.

# Entertainment

▼ In the evening a middle-class family might peer through a stereoscope which made two photographs magically appear in 3-D. If they tired of this, they might sing songs by the piano. Sheet music with bright covers was early pop music with hits like *The Great Exhibition Quadrille* or *Cook's Excursion Gallop* (which made fun of Thomas Cook's Italian excursion trips).

'Scientific' toys gave adults endless fascinating fun at home. Epidiascopes and magic lanterns projected flickering images onto walls; if you spun a Zoetrope (Wheel of Life) and looked through a slot, the pictures seemed to move. More complex toys had names to match, like phenakistoscope, praxinoscope, or zoopraxiscope. A Frenchman used one of these toys with an epidiascope to show moving pictures. Three years later, in 1895, the Lumière brothers astonished Paris with the first real movies, ten films lasting twenty minutes, twenty shows daily.

Most people could not such afford toys. They often relaxed in bars, cafés, or public houses. Others got dead drunk on poisonous brews in foul city dens. But in France and Britain, especially, singers were used to attract custom. This led to music halls where you could see magicians, boxers, comics, or strong-men. By the second half of the century, music hall stars were very popular with working people. London's Little Tich's silly dancing was famous across Europe. By 1890 *La Goulou* (The Glutton), dancing the can-can in a swirl of lace to blaring trombones and crashing drums and cymbals, or Valentin (*Le Désossé*, the Boneless One), with his weird contortions, helped make Paris the world's 'pleasure capital'. In 1886, New Yorkers hummed *You Naughty, Naughty Men*, a hit from the first musical.

You often heard music outside. It might be an Italian organ grinder with a monkey, or the sad tin whistle of a crippled soldier. You might even see a dancing bear – performing animals were very popular, especially at circuses: many cities had permanent buildings for circuses.

▼ In the 1870s new sports, like roller-skating, cycling and tennis became popular with healthy-minded middle-class people. Women joined in all of these, and so gained a little more freedom. Watching professional football became a common way for a working man in Britain to spend Saturday afternoon after 1880.

▲ Many theatres were very rowdy. People threw insults or rotten fruit at artists they did not like. Stage effects were often astonishing; 'ghosts' appeared by clever use of lights and mirrors; real horses raced and naval battles were fought with models in giant water tanks.

▼ Drink was often called 'the curse of the working class': many people became ill or died through alcohol. Men often spent their wages on drink whilst their wives and children went hungry. But after a hard day's work it was hard to relax in a dark, damp and cramped slum room. Drinking places, especially in Britain, were often colourful and gave relief from the misery of peoples' lives.

◄ The 'Greatest Show on Earth'– Barnum and Bailey's circus– comes to town! Its shows included Tom Thumb and his wife (both under one metre tall) and the 'Original Stupendous Historic and Spectacular Classic Destruction of Rome'. A rival 'tenting' circus had a three km procession with 70 horse-drawn waggons (20 carrying wild beasts), followed by show horses and 100 Shetland ponies. Elephants and camels ambled up behind. It took nine months to 'roll' over 3,000 km, giving two shows a day to 200 towns.

# Highdays and holidays

Poor people worked long days with no paid holidays. Sunday was usually free – and it might be the only day factory workers saw sunlight. Christmas and Easter were special holidays (though not so long as today) for all Christians and in Catholic countries saints' days were extra chances for rest days.

Most country towns had annual fairs where farmers sold or bought animals and wives sold home-made cloth. Farm workers looked for next year's job; deals were agreed over a drink. To the scrapings of a beggar's fiddle, you could munch spicey cakes or hot chestnuts, or try your luck catching a pig by its tail. Later, after many drinks and bargains, people danced noisily into the night.

Tourism was not new to the rich and it soon spread to the middle-classes. By 1851 Thomas Cook was running special railway excursions to the Crystal Palace. In 1864 he organised the first 'package tour' to Europe. His tourists read about the places they visited in new guidebooks published by a German, Karl Baedeker.

Excursions were more rough-and-tumble for the poor, but they too benefited from cheap fares; one 1840 train took 3,000 people in 67 carriages drawn by four engines.

▲ Going for a country picnic on an 1862 cheap excursion bus. Before cheap buses and railways, working people's travel was limited by how far they could walk. It was difficult to get away from the smoke and grime into the country.

► Tourists watched this French Catholic festival in Brittany (where they could also go bathing). For local peasants a saint's day was a chance to dress up in their best for a holiday. After the ceremonies there would be merry-making and a chance to meet the opposite sex. In Spain even the smallest town had a *fiesta,* when a town celebrated its saint's day with a holiday.

▼ Seaside holidays did not become popular until the last century when railways allowed townspeople to travel quickly and cheaply. This is Ramsgate in 1853.

People were very modest and sunbathing was unheard of— there would have been no danger of sun-burn! If they bathed, they changed in bathing machines (huts on wheels, on the far right) into long-sleeved costumes covering most of their bodies. The bathing machines were wheeled into the sea until bathers could slip into the water unnoticed. When the children got bored with paddling, they could watch a Punch and Judy show (above the man playing the drum in the centre). The child with the spade is wearing pantaloons.

# Religion

◄ This French painting, called *Sunday*, represents Heaven (the church) and Hell (the fiery furnace). It shows how church leaders hoped town workers would behave. Unfortunately, church leaders could no longer persuade people to go to church as regularly as they did in country villages. There were plenty of distractions in towns, like the inn in the lower left of the picture, to keep people away from church.

More realistically, some priests visited factories and mines to meet the workers. One German mine even had its own tiny church for its workers.

► Many church leaders realized that they could no longer rely on people attending church. Instead, the church had to go out to meet the people. These are Salvation Army officers holding an open-air service in London's streets.

In Africa and other parts of the world European church missionaries went out to try to convert natives to Christianity. Despite problems in Europe, Christianity was spreading through the world.

If you lived in 1800, you probably lived in the country, where the church was the centre of local life. You might go to a church school and you (and your parents and grandparents) might be baptized, married and buried at the same church. If you were sick or very poor, the church might help you with a little food or money.

But as people filled up the towns, they lost touch with their country churches. There was little to replace them. Later, many lofty Gothic churches were built, often in poor parts of towns, to attract people back to God. Inside, people sang rousing new hymns in the light from brightly coloured windows. But some, like the French Sisters of Charity and the Salvation Army, felt that the poor needed food and shelter as well as God's comfort—although they had to sing hymns or pray to get their soup. People like John Barnardo set up homes for orphans in Britain.

Factory owners who treated their workers like tools and

discarded them when they had no further use dismayed church-leaders; a German, for example, tried to stop night work for children. But though they saw evil in the towns, ideas of revolution alarmed the church leaders even more.

In most Christian countries, religion was in turmoil. Change had to come, but church leaders were unsure what to do. Many educated people became uncertain of their faith and of how much of the Bible they could really believe. In 1800 most people thought that the world was 6,000 years old. After the 1850s, however, scientists challenged such ideas and began a storm of of argument.

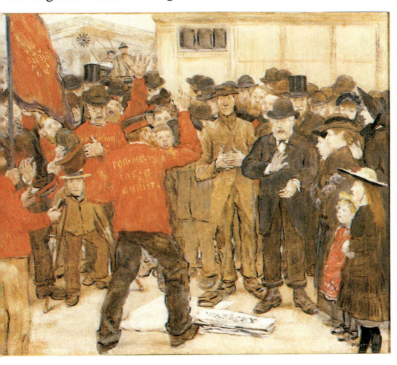

▼ A Russian Jew is hounded out of Kiev in 1881. Jews were viciously attacked in Eastern Europe. France was scandalized by an anti-Jewish plot against an army officer, Dreyfus.

Many Jews left Europe; in 1891 300,000 left Russia alone. The first Zionist congress in Switzerland in 1897 demanded a country in Palestine (now Israel) for all Jews where they could live in peace.

◄ Charles Darwin cartooned in 1874. He believed all animals *evolved* (very slowly developed) from simpler animals. Human beings evolved from apes. This idea outraged church-leaders—the Bible taught that God created every animal 'ready-made' in six days. Geologists, like Cuvier in France, realized that rocks contained fossil remains of extinct animals, whilst others showed that the earth's rocks were millions of years older than the Bible taught. In Vienna Sigmund Freud shocked people with his ideas about human behaviour. All these scientists undermined the teachings of churches.

# Warfare

Machines revolutionized wars. Some generals no longer even led their troops into battle. Von Moltke commanded his troops by telegraph from a Berlin desk. Generals had to understand railway timetables, for armies grew so big that only railways could move thousands of men (and their supplies) to arrive at the same place and time. A general did more organizing than fighting now.

Old rifles were muzzle-loaded. A soldier stood up and rammed the ball and powder down the barrel with a long rod. The guns were inaccurate and three shots a minute was a fast rate of fire. New breech-rifles were loaded in a slot in the barrel by the handle. A soldier could do this lying down in safety. Breech rifles also fired further and more rapidly. In 1862 Dr Gatling invented a machine gun which fired 700 shots a minute. As American Civil War soldiers discovered, one man armed with a machine gun could mow down hundreds of people.

In the same war, the warships *Merrimac* and *Monitor* fought the first 'ironclad' duel. The wooden sailing ship, at the wind's mercy, was on its way out. Like rifles, ships' cannons were changed to breech loaders.

The Battle of Solferino killed or wounded 39,000 men. Horrified by this, Dunant, a Swiss, helped start the Red Cross in 1864. It aimed to care for the wounded and prisoners in any war. Attempts to stop the international arms race in the 1890s were not so successful, but poison gas, at least, was banned. Apart from this, international rivalries and new military inventions led to bigger armies and more lethal weapons.

▲ Balloons were sometimes used to spy on enemy troops. This one was used during the siege of Paris during the Franco-Prussian war. It flew messages out of the city.

▼ War, like all other aspects of life, felt the effects of the Industrial Revolution. Nowhere was this more obvious than at sea. In 1800 fighting ships were wooden sailing ships that had hardly changed in centuries. By 1900 they were steam-driven monsters with thick steel armour and guns which could hurl huge shells over 18 kilometres. In the middle of the century, these two extremes overlapped in ships like *La Gloire*.

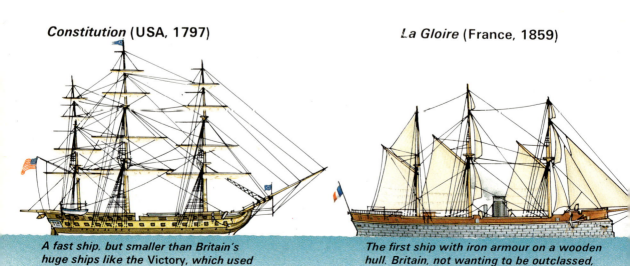

*Constitution* (USA, 1797)

*A fast ship, but smaller than Britain's huge ships like the* Victory, *which used about 2,000 oak trees to build it.*

*La Gloire* (France, 1859)

*The first ship with iron armour on a wooden hull. Britain, not wanting to be outclassed, built the first all iron warship in 1860.*

▲ Dead Americans on a Civil War battlefield. Most people thought war was a 'glorious thing'. To join a fashionable brigade was the ambition of many young men. Most battle paintings helped this belief, and they rarely showed the true picture. War photographs may have helped show people the shocking reality of war.

▶ Above all else, railways revolutionized land warfare. Wars speeded up because, instead of long, tiring marches, foot troops arrived quickly, fresh for battle. Germany first used railways successfully. Without railways, the huge armies of 1914 could not have moved.

*Potemkin* (Russia, 1900)

▼ An 1879 steam submarine. A submarine sank an enemy ship in 1863 in the American Civil War— unfortunately, it sank itself at the same time! Submarines were not yet practical, but by 1914 they were ready to sink hundreds of ships.

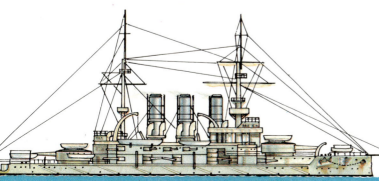

*A typical battleship of the time with 130 mm thick steel armour. As well as her guns, she had four torpedo tubes.*

# Revolutionaries

In the 1830s France, Belgium, Poland, Switzerland and parts of Germany and Italy were in revolt. 1848 and 1849 saw almost all of Europe explode into the bloodiest of violent revolutions. It was as if a gunpowder trail across Europe had blown up one country after another. The French Revolution of 1789 lit that gunpowder trail.

More people could read; cheap newpapers told them what their rulers were up to. Townspeople could easily go to meetings where fiery speakers could arouse thousands. Townspeople easily organized themselves into angry mobs.

Some revolutionaries were educated idealists, others were poor workers. Many were nationalists who hated foreign rulers. Often all these people joined together in revolt. It was confusing: rich and poor together fought foreigners, while poor people might fight against their own rulers. In the end, lack of unity caused most revolutions to fail. But the revolutions frightened the rulers. Gradually, they were forced to take more notice of people's demands.

German and British workers began cooperative societies to buy things more cheaply from factories. Elsewhere, farm co-ops bought and shared machinery; most Danish butter, eggs, cheese and bacon were produced cooperatively. Belgian co-ops ran shops, cafés and libraries. By 1890 trade unions were legal in most countries. Most unions helped skilled workers in sickness or death; they rarely struck for more pay. But in the 1880s and 1890s unions of less skilled workers struggled for more pay; French foresters, German miners, British match girls and dockers all fought bitter strikes. Working people were gaining strength together to fight their employers for better pay and working conditions.

▲ Karl Marx is the most important person in socialism's history. Helped by his friend, Friedrich Engels, he wrote masses of pamphlets and books about industrial countries. He thought that they automatically exploited working people and that the only way to stop this was for workers to seize power from their rulers. He wanted to see 'working men of all countries unite', for they had 'nothing to lose but their chains'. Marx said revolution would begin in the most industrial country–Britain. Instead, it was in backward Russia where peasants made the first successful socialist revolution in 1917.

▶ The last great Chartist meeting in 1848. Chartism was an idealistic British movement whose aims included votes for *all* men and annual general elections. It included intellectuals, but also workers who hated the factories, and hand-loom weavers whose jobs were threatened by the factories.

Some meetings were broken up by the army. But, by and large, British people had a little more freedom than most Europeans. It was enough to stop a British revolution in 1848.

◄ This French cartoon is ironically called *Liberty*. A fat, bloated capitalist (a factory owner and employer of workers), protected by soldiers, watches down-trodden workers trudge to work in his factory. Cartoons like this were meant to anger people into revolt.

▼ A street barricade in the Paris Commune. After France's defeat in the Franco-Prussian war, thousands of Parisians felt betrayed by their government and they revolted against it. For six weeks they held the city with barricaded roads. Government troops defeated them and killed or executed 30,000 *Communards*. Some revolutionary idealists were involved, but the Commune was not communist. It did, however, inspire revolutionaries to believe that a successful revolution was not far away.

► London dockers in 1871 protest against the treatment of fellow workers in the unsuccessful Paris Commune revolt. Many workers saw that their loyalties lay not with their bosses, church-leaders, or politicians, but with other workers. Improved communications and newspapers encouraged this feeling and in this case it even reached across the national boundaries.

# Nations old and new

People feel drawn towards other people who speak the same language and have similar customs. The French Revolution fanned feelings like this in Europe into a raging fire. The leaders of the revolution told French people that they must choose their ruler who must obey the people's will. It was as if millions of French people had drunk a strong brew that made them giddy with French pride. This brew is called nationalism. Many Europeans felt threatened by outsiders or were ruled by foreigners; thirstily, they too drank the powerful brew.

For example, in 1800 there was no such country as Italy. But people were beginning to see themselves as *Italians*, not Venetians, Romans or Neapolitans. After many struggles, when Italians fought Italians and Italians fought foreigners, Italy finally became a united country in 1870. Germany did

▼ Most European royal families were related to each other by birth or marriage. Queen Victoria was mother, grandmother or great grandmother to most of them. Victoria's grandchildren included the Czaritsa of Russia, the Queens of Romania and Norway, and Kaiser Wilhelm II. Here is Victoria (1) with more of her offspring: Princess Marie Louise of Schleswig Holstein (2); Princess Margaret, later Crown Princess of Sweden (3); the Duke of York, later Britain's King George V (4); Prince Albert of York, later Britain's King George VI (5); Princess Victoria Eugenie, later Queen of Spain (6).

▶ Queen Victoria ruled Britain from 1837 to 1901. She was very popular and was a symbol of the power and wealth of Britain and her empire. In her old age, people would drink a solemn Christmas toast to 'the dear old Queen'. Her Diamond Jubilee (60 years on the throne) was joyously celebrated—even the very poor were given free banquets. This photograph shows a shooting stall where you might win a Jubilee mug, or plate with the Queen's portrait on it.

not exist in 1800, either. But, led by Prussia, which had defeated Denmark, Austria and France, the 38 kingdoms and states were united into one country in 1871.

Elsewhere, nationalist feelings were stifled and this meant trouble. Inside the Turkish Empire, Muslims and Christians could not get on with each other. Greece and Roumania broke away and the empire became so rickety, that it was called the Sick Man of Europe. The Austro-Hungarian Empire was made up of a hotchpotch of nationalities including Poles, Slovaks, Italians, Hungarians and Czechs, all speaking different languages. Nationalist revolts constantly threatened the empire and parts of it broke away. Somehow, it survived. But not for long. Nationalism is a very powerful force; it destroyed the empire and devastated Europe in World War One.

▼ Franz-Josef (the policeman in this 1878 cartoon), ruler of the Austro-Hungarian Empire, tries to control two of his countries (the unruly children, Bosnia and Herzogovina). His empire included lots of different peoples who demanded their freedom from his hated rule. In 1914 things exploded when Franz-Josef's nephew was murdered in Bosnia by the man being arrested in the photograph. Two months later this led to World War One.

◄ To rousing military bands, loyal, enthusiastic Prussians show how proud they are to be Prussian by loudly cheering their king, Wilhelm, as he leaves Berlin to join his army in the war against France in 1870.

Five months later France surrendered and Germany became one nation. Prussia was the biggest and most powerful of the German kingdoms, so Wilhelm became Kaiser (Emperor) Wilhelm I of Germany.

# European empires

In 1800 Europe was losing control of much of the world it once owned. Early in the century, many countries could not be bothered with new empires. But gradually they began empire building and by 1900 Europe owned over 70% of the world. Even Belgium had a vast empire (80 times her size) in the Congo. King Leopold ran it as if it were his own personal property. Largest of all empires, Britain ruled 345,000,000 people and 28,000,000 square kilometres.

Empire building speeded up in the 1870s and 80s for many reasons. Missionaries, off to convert natives to Christianity, often arrived first. Traders in goods like gold, fur or diamonds might follow the missionaries. Many Dutch, French and British colonies were begun and run by companies like the East India Company which ruled India until 1858. The bloody Indian Mutiny made a reluctant British government take it over. Like it or not, countries had to protect their citizens abroad.

▲ Cecil Rhodes astride Africa. He dreamt of a railway, as well as the telegraph line he holds, linking north and south Africa from Cairo to the Cape. Rhodes helped Britain claim much of Africa – Rhodesia (Zimbabwe) was named after him. He once said he would colonize the planets if he could.

Many European countries took whatever land they could, even if it was useless. Often, it was just to stop others taking it first.

## 1880

## 1891

Who owned Africa?

## 1914

| | |
|---|---|
| 🟨 | Belgium |
| 🟩 | France |
| 🟥 | Britain |
| 🟪 | Spain |
| 🟧 | Germany |
| 🟫 | Portugal |
| 🟦 | Italy |
| ⬜ | Turkey |
| ⬜ | Unclaimed or unexplored |

Lake Victoria

Lake Tanganyika

Lake Nyasa

Madagascar

◄ Until the late 1800s, much of Africa was unexplored. But by 1880 a European 'scramble for Africa' had begun; these maps show what happened.

During the century Europeans extended their control of the rest of the world. Europe had ruled many countries earlier; Spain and Portugal had a huge South American empire, but they lost most of it by 1830. Most of India was British-run by 1800 and in the Far East, Holland and Britain had great power, whilst France ruled Vietnam. By 1914 Germany had become envious of European empires across the world–this was one of many causes of World War One.

Europeans sold their factory goods in their empires. For example, in one year Britain earned £8,000,000 from her empire (apart from India). But it cost £4,000,000 to run it and even more fighting to defend it. To guard her ships trading on the seas, Britain used places like the Falkland Isles and Malta to refuel her navy with coal and food.

Steamships rushed troops to crush native revolts with their superior technology. News of such 'heroic' deeds aroused nationalist pride in European voters. Even if governments could not really afford empires, they were popular with their voters. Governments were encouraged to snatch up any land that was available.

▼ African police. Europeans who ruled a country took their customs with them. Today Spanish is spoken where Spain once ruled, and where France ruled, you can still enjoy French cooking.

Natives employed by Europeans were poorly paid and badly treated. Belgian Congo Africans were treated like slaves.

▼ Settlers chase Australian aborigines off the land. Tribes suffered if they did not fit in with white settlers' plans for the land. Tasmanian aborigines were wiped out. Much of the USA was stolen from the Indians and thousands of them were killed. 60,000,000 bison, which the Indians used for food, clothing, tools and tents, were shot by settlers. If these sort of tactics failed, natives often died of settlers' diseases.

# New lives in new lands

▼ Steerage class for trans-Atlantic emigrants. It was described in 1847 as 'hundreds of poor people, men, women, and children, of all ages, from the drivelling idiot of ninety to the babe just born, huddled together, without light, without air, wallowing in filth and breathing a (foul) atmosphere, sick in body, dispirited in heart'. Food was bad, and in short supply; you took your own if you had money.

Steam ships cut crossings to ten days; life aboard was much better—even hot food was served! But steam travel cost more than twice as much.

The year was 1850. A tired, hungry farm worker relaxed at an inn. On a wall, a poster told him of 'ships of the largest class commanded by men of experience, who will take every precaution to promote the health and comfort of passengers' on the voyage. A friend of his had sent money from America and he had heard tales of free farmland out there. He needed to save £3.50 for the fare and as much again for food and clothes on the trip; his weekly wage was 35p. Once he was there, he could send tickets for his wife and children to follow him out to the new farm he would have. Nobody would be his boss and he might even buy a horse and carriage . . .

Many a new life abroad began like this. Europe had 210,000,000 more people in 1900 than in 1800, but there was not enough food, jobs and homes for them all. Until the

► Newly arrived Scandinavians wait at New York's landing station. Many immigrants came from very poor countries. New York, was a flashy, busy city. You could read long lists of New Yorkers worth $100,000 or more. Richest of all was J.J. Astor, who was once a poor immigrant himself. He had a fortune of $25,000,000. New immigrants dreamt of his sort of success. Instead, crooks often conned the ignorant peasants out of their tiny life savings as they landed.

1880s, mainly Irish, British and Germans risked the four to seven week long Atlantic trip. Few ships had doctors and many passengers died. One ship left Liverpool with 634 emigrants, but reached New York with only 476. After 1870, 21,000,000 Poles, Greeks, Hungarians, Italians or Jews, left Europe, half for the USA, the rest for New Zealand, Australia, Canada, South America or South Africa. Many, especially Jews, left Europe to escape religious or political persecution.

New York's Statue of Liberty (a gift from France in 1886) welcomed Europeans with the words 'Give me your tired, your poor, your huddled masses, yearning to breathe free'. But some Americans worried about the floods of new foreigners. They thought that Catholics, or people who spoke no English, or people who clung to European ways, were unAmerican and a threat to the country. Fears like this put a stop to Chinese emigrants after 1882.

◀ Australian gold fever in the 1850s. Life was so grim for many Europeans, that only dreams of a new life kept them going. Newspaper reports of gold finds in South Africa, the USA and Australia always produced extra rushes of hopeful immigrants. Few made their fortunes.

Australia was at first a dumping ground for British convicts. Few people cared for a 13,000 km sea trip, and Australia did not attract them. Steam ships, gold and news of rich farm land changed all that.

▶ A settlers' waggon train heads west across the Rockies. Many immigrants dreamt of a land of 'milk and honey' that was there for the taking in the Wild West. Most of the 29,500,000 Italians, Irish, Germans and British who arrived in eastern America could not afford the trek out west. Instead, they ended up working in America's booming factories.

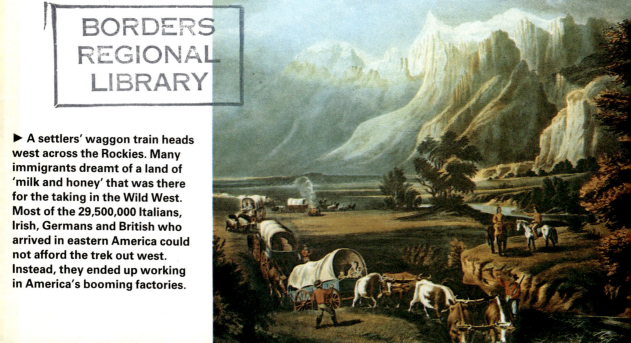

# Main events

**1801** United Kingdom formed by union of Great Britain and Northern Ireland.

**1802** *Charlotte Dundas*, the first steamship, sails on the Clyde river in Scotland.

**1804** Napoleon Bonaparte crowns himself emperor of the French.
First experimental steam locomotive runs on rails in England.

**1805** Battle of Trafalgar won by Britain over France.

**1807** Slavery abolished in British Empire.

**1812** Napoleon invades Russia

**1814** Napoleon abdicates from throne.

**1815** Battle of Waterloo.
Napoleon exiled to St Helena.

**1816** Argentina gains freedom from Spain.

**1819** 'Macadam' roads laid in Britain.

**1821** Greek War of Independence against Turkey begins.

**1823** 'Monroe Doctrine' announced by USA; Europe told not to interfere in South America.
'Macintosh' – waterproof material – invented by Charles Macintosh.

**1824** Beethoven finishes ninth symphony.

**1825** Erie Canal links New York with the Great Lakes, 520 km away.

**1830** Charles X, King of France, deposed.

**1832** Electric telegraph invented. Samuel Morse develops his code for it.
Greece becomes independent of Turkey.

**1835** The 'Great Trek' of the Boers begins in South Africa.

**1837** Victoria becomes Queen of Britain.

**1840** Antarctic coast discovered.
Rowland Hill begins 'Penny Post'.

**1845** Submarine telegraph cable laid between France and England.

**1846** Potato famine begins in Ireland.

**1847** Chloroform used successfully for the first time as an anaesthetic.

**1848** The 'Year of Revolutions': France, Austria, Italy, Croatia, Germany and Sicily all experience revolts.
Gold rush in California.
First settlers in New Zealand.
Marx publishes *Communist Manifesto*.

**1849** David Livingstone begins exploration in Africa.

**1851** Gold rush in Australia.
Great Exhibition opens in London.

**1854** America opens up Japan to trade with the rest of the world.

**1854** Crimean War between Russia and the Allies (France, Britain, Turkey and Sardinia).

**1855** Florence Nightingale begins hospital reform in Scutari, Turkey.

**1856** Henry Bessemer invents a 'converter' to make steel cheaply from iron.

**1857** Indian Mutiny.

**1858** First trans-Atlantic telegraph cable laid.

**1859** Darwin publishes *Origin of Species*.
Petroleum found in Pennsylvania, USA; used for heating and lighting.

**1861** Serfs emancipated in Russia.
American Civil War begins.

**1863** First underground railway in London.

**1864** War between Denmark and Prussia.
International Red Cross founded.

**1865** American Civil War ends. Lincoln, president of USA, assassinated.
Frenchman, Jules Verne, writes *Earth to the Moon* about a trip to the moon.

**1867** Alfred Nobel invents dynamite; later founds Nobel Prizes for peace, physics, chemistry, medicine and literature.
Alaska bought by USA for $7,200,000 from Russia.

**1869** Suez Canal opens.
Transcontinental Railroad completed in USA.

**1870** The Pope declares himself to be 'infallible' and can make no mistakes about morals or faith.

**1871** Zanzibar slave market closed through British pressure.

Italy unified.

German Empire founded.

Paris Commune set up, but fails later.

**1874** Factory Act in Britain limits hours of work.

Typewriter invented.

**1875** Britain buys Egyptian share of Suez Canal and increases her control of it.

**1876** First railway in China.

Telephone invented.

First motor car runs.

**1877** First frozen meat cargo arrives in Britain from Argentina.

Edison patents cylinder phonograph (early gramophone).

**1880** Discovery of cause of malaria.

**1881** Pasteur successfully immunizes people against anthrax.

Czar Alexander II of Russia assassinated by members of the 'People's Freedom Group'.

**1884** Rules for taking over Africa drawn up by European countries at Berlin.

Machine gun invented by Maxim.

**1885** National Congress formed in India as first step to India's independence.

**1888** Pneumatic tyre invented by Dunlop.

Greenland ice-cap crossed.

**1889** Eiffel Tower built.

**1891** Trans-Siberian railway begun.

**1893** British acquire Uganda.

**1894** Moving pictures (cinematograph) invented by Lumiére brothers.

**1895** X-rays discovered.

Kiel canal opened in Germany.

**1896** Marconi invents wireless telegraphy.

**1898** Pierre and Marie Curie discover the effects of radium.

Spanish-American War: USA acquires Phillipine Islands.

**1899** Boer War begins.

**Prince Albert** was Queen Victoria's beloved German husband. His death from typhoid in 1861 devastated Victoria with grief.

**Phineas T. Barnum** was a brash American with a gift for publicity stunts and exaggerated claims for his shows and circuses.

**Isabella Beeton** (1833-65) wrote cookery books that sold 2,000,000 copies in the first ten years.

**Amelia Bloomer** (1828-94) was an American who fought for women's rights, despite people's ridicule.

**Isambard Kingdom Brunel** (1806-59) was a British engineer, killed by over work. He built ships, tunnels, bridges and railways.

**Gustave Eiffel** (1832-1923), a French engineer, built the Eiffel Tower as well as bridges and a frame in the Statue of Liberty.

**Sigmund Freud** (1856-1939), an Austrian, whose *Interpretation of Dreams* began the scientific study of human behaviour.

**Baron Haussman** (1809-91) demolished much of old Paris and rebuilt it with wide streets that could not be easily barricaded.

**Joseph Lister** (1827-1912) made a breakthrough by discovering that carbolic acid kills germs.

**Alfred Krupp** (1812-1887) turned a small iron works into Germany's giant Ruhr steel and armaments factories.

**Florence Nightingale** (1820-1910) fought to become a nurse. She brilliantly reorganized the Crimean hospitals.

**Louis Pasteur** (1822-95) made the major discovery of how germs are passed on.

**Helmuth von Moltke** (1800-91), a Prussian military genius, whose plans and use of railways crushed Austria-Hungary and France.

**George Stephenson** (1781-1848) built the first reliable steam locomotive for a public railway. He also built railway lines.

**James Watt** (1736-1819) was a Scot who greatly improved the steam engine. Many worked in factories or mines.

# Glossary Index

**American Civil War** It was fought between 11 Southern states (which wanted to break away from the USA) and the rest of the Northern states. One cause was slavery: the South wanted it, the North did not. A million people died before the South was defeated.

**Austro-Hungarian Empire** The ancient Habsburg empire once ruled much of Europe. By 1867 its Viennese rulers were losing control of the empire: a compromise was reached with one of the strongest peoples in the empire, the Hungarians, to share power. The empire was now called the Austro-Hungarian Empire. As well as Austria and Hungary, it included parts of today's Italy, Jugoslavia, Romania, Poland and Czechoslovakia.

**emigrants** People who leave one country to live in another.

**Franco-Prussian War** France and Prussia were rivals, and this led to war. France lost Alsace and Lorraine to the Prussian victors.

**immigrants** People living in one country who were born in another.

**middle-class** People not so rich as the upper-classes, but who could afford things like their own houses. Most were well educated. They included army and navy officers, vicars and priests, teachers, but mainly businessmen.

**upper-** and **ruling-classes** The richest and most powerful people who controlled, or ruled people's lives. They included kings or queens, politicians, bishops, rich businessmen and army and navy commanders.

**Victorians** Queen Victoria ruled Britain for so much of the century, that 19th century people are often called Victorians.

**working-class** There were more of these people than any other class. They were poor and usually could not afford to own houses. They were often badly educated. They included farm and factory workers, servants, shopworkers and ordinary sailors and soldiers.